NEVER TURN BACK

THE TESTIMONY OF

FRANCISCO CORTEZ

SHACKLES TO FREEDOM

ISBN: 979-8-8693-6515-6

1st Edition, Published in the United States of America by Shackles to Freedom.

Cover art, interior layout, and transcription by Kelby Losack
kelbylosack.com

Printed in the USA

1

"Thus sayeth the Lord, 'Stand at the crossroads and look; ask for the ancient paths, ask where the good way is, and walk in it, and you will find rest for your soul.'" – Jeremiah 6:16

TATTOOED ON MY CHEST is the ouroboros—a serpent eating its own tail, forming a perfect circle. Or, in my case, an incomplete circle. The tattoo, now old and faded, was never finished.

A completed circle has no beginning and no end. To the Mexican mafia, this tattoo means you're in *la familia* for life.

I knew there would be consequences for wanting to walk away.

They called me to the home of a Lieutenant down in Freeport, Texas. *Mi padrino*—the man who'd brought me into the mafia—drove me there. There were guards posted out front of the house, watching the street.

We sat parked at the curb for a minute, not saying anything, letting everything that could have been said just hang in the air.

Then my padrino said, "Well," and he cut the engine, and my chest went flat as my lungs deflated, and he said, "This is it."

All eyes were on us as soon as we stepped inside. *Pistoleros* posted up in every corner. The Captain, who'd come down from Houston, stood over at the bar along with the Lieutenant. Guns laid out across the bar. I locked eyes with the Captain and walked towards him, my heart on my tongue and my shoes full of cement. The room seemed to stretch out, as if the bar was suddenly a mile off in the distance, the men with their drinks and their guns just specks on the horizon. Halfway across the impossibly large room, I heard the echo of the Captain's voice, muffled under the sound of my own pulse.

"Stop," he said.

And so I stopped. I stood there, surrounded by pistoleros, my padrino at my back, Lieutenant and Captain with their eyes locked on mine.

The Captain said, "There's something different about you."

I swallowed the lump in my throat and said to him, "I had an encounter with God. I am not the same as I once was."

There was a long pause as he looked me up and down.

"I believe you," he said. "There is a glow all over you."

He motioned at the empty barstools and told us to sit, and so we did—the Captain, the Lieutenant, my padrino, and me. The Captain and Lieutenant asked us both a bunch of questions, then said for us to go. They said I was to come back the following day, and they said to return alone.

It rattled me a bit, back in the car, seeing my padrino's eyes well up with tears. The way this was about to go down was, after hearing my petition to leave, they were going to hold a vote. Let me walk or take me out. If it turned out to be the latter, my padrino would have to be the one to see to it, since he's the one who had brought me in.

"You could run," he said. "Off to some other state. Never come back."

"I'm at peace with this," I told him. "Either God will change their hearts, or they'll take my life. But it's all in His hands."

As I said this to him, I believed it. I'd given my life to the Lord, and now—as a Sargeant in the Mexican mafia—I'd made peace with whatever was to come of that.

When I returned the next day, the only ones in the room were two pistoleros in their corners and the Captain by the bar.

The Captain said, "Sit." And when I sat, only half-asking, he said, "Your mind is made up?"

"It is," I said to him. "I've given my life to the Lord."

"I have no interest in going to war with God," the Captain said.

Thing about the Mexican mafia is most of them are very religious, in their own way.

"We put it up to a vote," he said, and at this point, even though I'd made my peace, my palms were sweating and my heart was pounding again. The

Captain went on: "Either we let you walk, assuming you are being truthful and we won't have to kill you for joining another family, or we save ourselves the trouble of worrying over it and kill you now."

I said nothing. I looked the Captain in the eyes and awaited my fate.

There were three votes cast.

Two voted one way, one voted against them.

And by a matter of one vote, I was allowed to walk.

The Captain was one of the two who voted to let me go. "It's the glow I'm seeing on you," he said. "Something has changed. I don't want the repercussions of standing in God's way of what He's doing with you."

And like that, God had pulled me out of a place I should have never been allowed to leave.

2

"For I know the plans I have for you," declares the Lord, "plans to prosper you and not to harm you, plans to give you hope and a future." - Jeremiah 29:11

RACINE, WISCONSIN IS WHERE I was born into the struggle. Mom's only boy, the middle child between two sisters. My mom was a hard worker, always juggling two or three jobs to put food on the table. We were all over the place as kids, traveling up and down the country while my mom worked this or that job—my sisters and I tagging along to pick tomatoes and cherries up in Michigan—until eventually, she chased the next payday back to Bay City, Texas, where the rest of our family lived.

Well, okay, maybe it was an incident in which me and my sisters disappeared on one of these vegetable-picking trips that freaked my mom out and made her decide to move back around family.

My mom's folks had grown up in the Great Depression, and instilled a solid work ethic in my mom from a young age. But my sisters and me, we preferred to throw cherries and tomatoes at each other and then run off to fall asleep somewhere in the rows of crops.

My sisters and I were raised to believe in God, we attended Sunday school and all that, but the weight of the world—the way I saw my mom grinding and sacrificing to care for us, and all the duties it took to raise a family—those were the lessons I was taking in the most.

Early on, my outlook on life came with a heavy burden of responsibility for my family.

In seventh grade, I felt more needed at home than in school, so I dropped out.

My mom had a thing against babysitters ever since this one time, my babysitter took some pictures of me with my clothes off, and when Mom found out, let me tell you, she tore that babysitter *up*. The laws came and arrested my babysitter and after that, my mom didn't believe in hiring anyone to look after any of us. So, from then on, it was on me to look after my sisters.

Inside me through all this was a constant battle to not turn out like my father, who my mom had kicked to the curb when I was real young. He was abusive to her, always trying to break her down mentally and just being plain ugly to her, and while I wasn't like him in *those* ways, I *was* a fighter. A hyper kid with an attention disorder and a rebellious nature.

When I started smoking weed around age twelve, it was like I had finally found something to calm me down, quiet the noise in my head, make me feel normal.

At some point, that mellow high wasn't enough, and I started experimenting with harder drugs.

Growing up with cousins and friends who were always running the streets, it was easy to get into such vices at an early age. It wasn't even that I didn't have good influences. My mom ended up marrying this guy Adam, and Adam had always been a great role model. Since they first started dating, he'd often take us kids out along with my mom to show he cared for *all* of us. Treated us like his own.

Adam showed me how to work, but encouraged me to be a kid, too.

And then my grandmother, she was always telling me, "Son, God has something special in store for you," but this would go in one ear and out the other.

I wasn't carrying hatred in my heart, I just didn't want to listen to what anyone had to say. I had love from my family, I knew who God was, but I was on Frankie's time. I wanted to do *me*. And it was so much easier to run the streets than to take responsibility. I had experienced pain so early on and spent a lot of my childhood craving ways to numb it, to make it go away. In my mind, there was no future for me—no way out of the cycle of struggle, no escape from the chaos in my head—so I lived each day as if there'd be no tomorrow.

3

"...for all have sinned and fall short of the glory of God, and all are justified freely by his grace through the redemption that came by Christ Jesus." - Romans 3:23-24

I F GOD DIDN'T ANSWER prayer, I might not have lived past sixteen. I had a relationship with God at this time, sure. I was always praying.

"Please, God, heal my earache."

"Please, God, don't let Mom find out about last night."

"This party tonight is going to be a wild one, God, please help me make it back home."

There were at least a couple incidents where I *shouldn't* have made it back home.

Like this one time, at a quinceañera in Bay City, a man disrespected my sister and so I got a group of some friends and cousins together and we followed the man out to his car as he was leaving and we beat on him through the window.

Arms everywhere, reaching in through the driver's side window to wail on this guy, tugging at his shirt collar while he spun the wheel back and forth, trying to shake us off or run us over.

Finally, the man floored it and took off. Then my sister, her boyfriend, and I went to a party at his house.

He hadn't made it there yet.

Maybe we were aware it was his house and didn't care, maybe we didn't even know, I don't remember. Partying was just what we did. We went where everyone else was going, wherever teenagers might be able to get drunk or high. Well, the guy eventually shows up of course, and when he sees us there, he starts hollering he's going to shoot us.

We knew he was serious when he pulled a gun out and started waving it around, still shouting.

There were a few trees out in the yard. I ran at the guy, ducking from tree to tree. He squeezed a few shots off in my direction, each of them a miss. I made it to him without so much as a graze on the arm.

Another time, leaving this place down in Old Ocean, I was drunk and driving way too fast. There were six of us piled in the Ford Explorer. Took a curve too sharply outside Sweeny, out where the ditches are so deep you'd have to climb out the bottom of them.

It'd been raining, so the ditches were full of water.

When the tires left the road, everything went into slow motion. We tumbled through the air, junk food wrappers and loose change floating around the cab like we'd blasted off into zero gravity. One of our friends in the back knocked his head against the window or something, went unconscious.

We rolled upside down, then all the way over, and nosedived into a flooded ditch. Water started pouring in through the cracks in the door seals.

We climbed over each other to the back window and kicked it out, then we piled out onto the sky-facing hatch of the Explorer. Then we reached in and grabbed our knocked-out friend by the armpits and dragged him out, too. We were drenched, panicked, a little whiplashed.

But we were alive, all of us.

I was stealing for money at this time. Breaking into homes. Caught probation for hitting this one place we thought was vacant. We'd broken the door down, not realizing someone was inside, sleeping. We took off running fast as we could, but it wasn't fast enough.

I say that last part to say this: If God didn't have a purpose for each of His children, what was He doing keeping His hands of protection on a street punk who was getting high and breaking into homes down in Gulf Coast Texas?

4

---

*"Behold, I set before you the way
of life and the way of death." –
Jeremiah 21:8*

I GOT A GIRL pregnant around that same time. We weren't really going together, just a fling type of thing. Her grandmother was the one to share the news. Stopped by the house one day to tell us her granddaughter was pregnant. My mom was not too happy about this.

The girl was a drug addict. Nobody thought she'd be good to take care of a kid, not even her own family. And me—I was in no position to make that kind of judgement, no position to be raising a kid either. I was still a kid myself.

I showed up to the hospital, though, when that day came. I was there for my son being born, before he was given over to be raised by his grandmother.

It wasn't long after bringing a new life into the world that I'd be going to prison for taking out another one.

It was New Year's Eve. I was eighteen. Told my mom I was heading out to this party in Wharton. When I told her exactly where, she begged me not to go. The people throwing this party had some beef with my uncles. They'd gotten into a big fight with each other a couple years back.

I told my mom, "That's ancient history, water under the bridge. You're worrying over nothing."

She wasn't convinced. "Please, do not go to this party," she said.

But I wasn't listening.

I've always been a dancer. I love to dance. So at the party, I grab a girl to dance with, and we're having a good time—just music and good party vibes, Happy New Year and all that—until the boyfriend of the girl I'm dancing with walks up to interrupt us. I told him I didn't want any trouble, you know, just having a good time. He said he didn't want any trouble either, but then he took a good look at me and asked if I was related to these guys he knew.

My uncles.

I took that as a good sign to leave. Made it out of the party with no drama.

My family ushered in the New Year at my aunt's place, playing cards in the kitchen. That's what we were up to at two in the morning when someone knocked on the door. I went to answer it and was then face to face with the guy from Wharton—the buzzkill boyfriend.

He was there on the porch with a big group of other guys from the party.

One of them said, "You're gonna die tonight!"

They jumped me. They beat on me from the front door all the way out to the yard.

My family came running out, screaming and hollering, and soon as I could, I slipped my hand in my pocket and took out this knife I liked to keep on me. Adrenaline had my head pounding. This was the opposite of the car crash, everything was speeding up. I was moving in fast forward.

I stabbed four of them.

They took off.

I remember it was very cold that night. The type of cold where it's hard to tell how badly you're beaten. If the guys who jumped me had run off to the hospital instead of another party, maybe things would have been different, but as it went down, one of the guys I stabbed died from his wounds a little later on.

Four in the morning, the police came by, and I explained to them what happened.

Apparently, the other family was going around looking for me, so my family hid me.

I took off to California, wanted for murder.

5

"The Lord sets prisoners free." –
Psalm 146:7

THE RUNNING, THE HIDING—IT ate at me. Ate at my spirit. For two years, I was on the run, until I decided to go back to Texas and turn myself in.

This was 1989. I was twenty years old now, facing a fourteen-year sentence for a split-second decision.

Day one in prison, the intake officers were betting each other how long it'd take for me to get roughed up. Their jaws dropped once I made it into general population and was immediately recognized, welcomed by family. I had barely gotten my feet wet before I was approached about joining the Mexican mafia.

I was appointed the role of Sargeant, which basically meant I did whatever the Captain ordered. I was in charge of my block—about twenty men—and it was my duty to collect money, drugs, things like that to spread amongst the soldiers. One thing I learned about prison is it was even easier to get drugs in there than on the streets.

Even locked up, I still went to church every Sunday.

Had to.

Chapel was where the Mexican mafia held meetings.

One meeting, this evangelist had come to preach. After the sermon, we were gathered in a circle—us soldiers, I mean—and the evangelist came up to me directly. As a leader in the Mexican mafia, people don't just walk up to you, that's not a thing you're used to.

In that moment, time stood still.

Several seconds of silence stretched on for a lifetime as we all just stared at this man of God.

He stood in the middle of our circle and said to me, "The Lord wanted me to tell you something. You won't understand it now, but one day you will. He wanted me to tell you, He's got a purpose for your life."

My last two years in there, I'd spent in solitary, which meant a small cell to myself behind a steel door and minimal face-to-face interaction with anybody. Days were made up of twenty-three hours in the cell, one hour of rec time. We had to shout at each other through the walls to keep from going crazy. All day long, a cacophony of faceless voices, like living with the loudest ghosts to ever haunt a place.

Only time the block would shut up was when the chaplain came to visit.

When the chaplain showed up, that meant one thing: someone was about to hear a loved one died. It was after a visit from the chaplain, one of the inmates hung himself in his cell.

Something I'll never forget about solitary—no matter how hard anyone acted, what you'd hear every night were the sounds of men praying and crying themselves to sleep.

Time doesn't exist the same way behind bars. Life on the inside must have slipped by, because before I knew it—six years into my sentence—I'd made parole.

It was June 1995. The Spurs were playing the Rockets. A group of us were using our one hour to huddle around the TV, lost in all the excitement of the game, when one of the guards came up to tell me I was going home.

Besides just shouting at each other through the walls, we'd cast lines of string through the food tray slots, and we'd pass the lines down the row to trade cigarettes, letters—whatever. I've always been a chatter box, and you better believe the night I found out I'd be going home, I couldn't stop running my mouth. That is, until I heard one of the guards shout, "Cortez! If you don't shut up right now, you'll be spending another six months in here!"

I shut my mouth without a second thought, and I was so quiet the rest of the night, you could hear a cockroach's footsteps.

A letter made its way over to my cell from one of the other inmates. I took it off the string and unfolded it. It said, NEVER TURN BACK.

It was a reminder.

See, what happened when you were finally released, is you were given a hundred dollars and a bus ticket, and then you had to make the longest walk of your life down this corridor leading up to what they called the Golden Gates, even though they were made of brass. And it's said that as you make this long walk back to freedom, it's bad luck to look back even once. To turn back, you'd be cursing yourself to get locked up again someday.

I took that walk to the Golden Gates, and I never turned back.

6

"Immediately there fell from his eyes something like scales, and he received his sight at once; and he arose and was baptized." - Acts 9:18

FRESH OUT OF PRISON, I was staying in a mobile home near the ball field in Brazoria. Same things I had been doing on the inside, I fell right back into on the outside, only now—with my freedom back—I could get into even more trouble.

During this time, I got a job at Dollar General. There was a man who worked there who would always be praying on his lunch breaks. One day, he asks me to join him for lunch, and I say to him, "Okay, man, but look, I don't want to hear anything about God or any of that." The man says, "We ain't gotta talk about any of that." He's just being friendly, offering some company. So I say, "Yeah, that sounds good."

Walking out to the parking lot with him, though, I got this feeling, like a wave of energy that hit me so hard I could barely move. It was like when you swim way out in the ocean and hit a sandbar, and you're exhausted from swimming, but there's ground beneath your feet again and so you plant your feet and try to catch your breath, but even that ground is moving, slowly, the sand slipping with the current and tugging you back while the waves are also pushing you around, and it's all overwhelming—all this motion swirling around you and beneath you, pushing at you—and not just that, but there's the taste of salt in the air, the smell of fish, and it's too much to take in all at once and so what you do is you fight to simply remain still. You channel all your strength into remaining grounded until you can adjust to the chaos swirling around you. And then once you do—once you finally adjust and you can stand there without fighting the waves or the current—you're awe-struck by the grand majesty of it all.

That's what the presence of God feels like, and that's what I felt that day walking out to the parking lot at Dollar General with Mr. Prays-a-Lot. When I could catch myself and breathe for a moment, I felt this assurance—not an audible voice, but a message I could just feel in my head, in my gut, in my heart—telling me over and over that I could be forgiven. It was so powerful, I cried for days.

This experience pushed me to seek out the nearest church, which was Brazoria First Assembly. At this time, most of the men in the congregation were away at a revival in Pensacola, and the church was having a special prayer service. I showed up wearing a bright red shirt, thinking I could keep quiet and to myself in the back row.

Since first stepping foot inside the church, though, there'd been something stirring in my gut, rattling my bones. It was that presence again, the same overwhelming presence I felt in the Dollar General parking lot, and apparently, I was doing a terrible job of hiding it, because a woman in the choir named Jackie spotted me from the stage. She set down her microphone and walked down the aisle to where I was sitting. She said the Lord spoke to her about me. She came by to ask if I was okay.

I shook my head. "No," I told her. "I am not okay."

She went and got the pastor, Pastor Ron Hogan, to come pray with me, and I let it all go right there. I fell to my knees and accepted Jesus into my life.

7

"For this purpose also I labor, striving according to His power, which mightily works within me." - Colossians 1:29

IT WAS THEN I decided to leave the Mexican mafia to begin chasing after whatever it was God was wanting me to do. Even after they barely let me out, though, the change wasn't something that happened overnight. Life would ebb and flow between new opportunities and old habits.

I went through two divorces and found out a girl I'd been told way back was not my child was, in fact, my daughter.

When it came to my walk with the Lord, I was definitely wobbling around on sea legs, but God moved me in the direction of people to help guide me. Deke Grovesnor, a car salesman and a good friend, would always invite me to church. Kenny Stanford gave me a job at his woodshop and would minister to me every day. I started sharing my testimony anywhere I could. I knew there were things I needed to cut out, but I was still getting high. If God was working through me, He must have been getting a good workout, because I certainly wasn't making things easy.

One day, working for Kenny, I was told to mow the vacant lot next to the shop. I had a good high going that morning, and all I had to do was mow this big square patch of grass. Sounded like a nice, easy start to the day, and that it was, until Kenny called me over to him, waving his hand across his neck for me to cut the mower.

He was trying to hide a smile and the redness in his face that would give away how hard he'd been laughing, and he asked me, "Frankie, what are you doing?"

Confused, I looked down at the John Deere I was sitting on, then looked out at the lot, then looked back to Kenny and said, "You told me to mow."

"Yeah," he said. "Think you oughtta turn the blades on?"

I took a closer look at the perimeter of grass I'd just driven and realized it was still the same height as everywhere I'd yet to pass over.

I was sent home for the rest of that day.

8

"Two are better than one, because they have a good return for their labor: If either of them falls down, one can help the other up." - Ecclesiastes 4:9-10

I MANAGED TO KEEP holding down the job at the woodshop. Every morning, Kenny would send me to get breakfast tacos from this restaurant whose idea of a breakfast taco was cold shredded cheese sprinkled over the blandest eggs, untouched by even a dash of pepper, slathered in pasty frijoles the consistency of generic bean dip, and rolled up in store-bought tortillas.

Finally, one day, I told him, "Look, if you want me to go and pick up tacos every morning, why don't you build a place, and I'll make the tacos."

And that's what happened. Ramon's Taquito Express opened up, and my next job for Kenny Stanford was also my next step in ministry, which all took place in the kitchen. I still held onto all the cooking skills I'd picked up from my mom, who actually ended up cooking along with me at Ramon's. We cranked out the best Mexican food West Columbia, Texas had ever known. It became a place the town gravitated to for community, for bonding over delicious meals whipped up fresh with love. This is where I learned that finding little ways to testify can have a big effect on the community. We would seal to-go wrappers with stickers that had inspirational scriptures printed on them. There were several occasions someone pulling through the drive-thru would want us to pray with them. We helped to cultivate a positive spirit that radiated through the town, which was more evidence to me that people can feel God anywhere. In the most subtle of gestures, like a sticker on a taco wrapper, God can move inside a whole town of people.

Around this same time, I married my wife of over twenty years now. Boy, that was a battle at first. We were two people so right for each other that of course we came with our own baggage. But the biggest blessings in life are always given through overcoming the biggest challenges.

I left Ramon's when my wife and I decided to try our hand at opening our own restaurant. That lasted about a year before we worked out a way to take up Kenny's offer on buying Ramon's.

Even with all the good things going on—a marriage to an amazing woman... owning a business... making an impact on our community—even trying to do right by God and lead a life following Christ, I *still* struggled with addictions.

9

"Trust in the Lord with all your heart, and lean not on your own understanding; in all your ways acknowledge Him, and He shall direct your paths." - Proverbs 3:5-6

P ETER WAS A MAN of little faith, and yet he was the first of Christ's disciples. In the face of a miracle—of Jesus walking across the water's surface during a storm, and then Peter himself stepping out on top of the water to meet him—Peter wavered. He went under. But the Son of God reached out to pull him back up. As he faced trial and crucifixion, Jesus also experienced the betrayal of Peter, who denied—*three times*—having ever even known him. Even still, after Christ's resurrection, the first disciple he went to visit was Peter.

A life committed to following Christ is by no means a life free of doubt or struggle.

My personal experience with the healing hand of God started with a severe headache. My wife closed up the restaurant while I went home to take some Tylenol PM and pass out. I woke up in the middle of the night, crawling on all fours to the bathroom to vomit up blood.

My wife carried me to the car and drove us to Brazosport Memorial Hospital. Leaning against her as we walked up to the sliding doors, I swayed, stumbled, collapsed into a flower bed. With a crown of crushed tulip pedals and my face streaked with mulch, they checked me in long enough to administer a spinal tap before life-flighting me to Galveston, where I was in SICU for seven days. I was told that the intense headache I'd been feeling was an aneurysm, and that I needed surgery.

Before any of that was set up, a doctor came in to speak with me.

"Do you believe in God?" she asked.

I said, "Yes."

She said God told her not to touch me, that He was healing me.

I'd been lying there, paralyzed, in the most extreme pain I'd ever felt, and now this doctor, she's telling me she can perform this surgery, and that logically she should, but that I have the right to refuse.

God was healing me, she'd said.

He spoke to her and said not to touch me.

I told the doctor, "I refuse surgery."

Four days later, I was out of the hospital.

I went straight to the altar at Brazoria First Assembly, the place I'd accepted Jesus into my life, and I lay there for hours.

We were hit with financial pitfalls at this time. We lost the restaurant. We lost nearly everything. But by the grace of God, and often by the skin of our teeth, we made it.

In the midst of the storm, you can either focus on the waves crashing over you, rocking your boat so violently back and forth that you're sure to be thrown over, or you can look out through the wind and the rain and find Jesus out there, walking on the water, the calm in the storm, calling out to you to come, just keep your eyes on him, and no matter how bad it gets, he won't let you go under.

10

"Repent, then, and turn to God, so that your sins may be wiped out."
- Acts 3:19

MY WHOLE LIFE HAS been a journey of miracles. The aneurysm was one wake-up call in what, looking back, feels like a lifetime of wake-up calls. So why so many chances? What purpose did God have for me that was so grand He would never give up?

When it comes to salvation and redemption stories, a lot of people look for the turning point, the road-to-Damascus moment. Saul becomes Paul. Mafia member becomes minister. But the true salvation moment is realizing God has been working inside of you the entire time, through every mistake or heartbreak, every setback, every tribulation.

Every struggle I lived through, God was there. He didn't show up suddenly in the hospital, or in the back row of First Assembly. He was there when I crashed that car, when I broke into that house, when I was in prison.

He was there when I was a child, when I first tried drugs, when I was taken advantage of by my babysitter.

He was there when I dropped out of school, thinking I had no future, but also thinking I had to be the man of the house.

He was there through my confusion, my bad decisions, my addictions.

He wasn't there keeping tabs on me, tallying up a debt that He'd come to collect on one day. He was simply there, waiting. Waiting for me to reach out to Him. Allowing me to fall on my own, but always ready to pick me up when I'd fallen too hard.

When I wanted to leave the Mexican mafia to serve the Lord, there was a vote to either let me go... or take my life.

By one vote, I was allowed to leave.

By one vote, I am still here today.

God can't force us to give our lives up to Him. He can't force us to change our ways. He can only be there, waiting for us to realize all the chances we've been given, for us to open our eyes and see the miracles that have been carrying us through our entire lives. No matter how hard we fall, and no matter how many times, He is still there, pulling us up, redirecting our steps back onto the path He's carved out for us. Living through the struggles and realizing God was there the whole time, that is the road-to-Damascus moment.

The moment the scales fall off the eyes, and we see God is right there, has been there, will always be there… so long as we choose to look to Him.

That's all God is waiting for.

Salvation is simply living with our eyes open.

After my aneurysm, after God's miraculous healing, after losing the restaurant, after an old church friend helped get me into selling cars, after being called into the ministry under the same pastor who I would eventually see buried on my birthday, each blessing has come with a challenge.

I found that my purpose had been going through all of these things so that I could help others with similar experiences and struggles. It's not too late for any of us. None of us are too far gone to realize that God is still right there before us, waiting with open arms. He's the same God who is the reason we've made it this far.

Let's open our eyes.

> *"Lord, have mercy on me, a sinner. I have done many things that don't please you in living my life only for myself. I believe that you died on the cross so that I may repent and be forgiven, and so I repent, and I ask you to please forgive me. From this day forward, I surrender my life to you. Help me to live every day in a way that pleases you and reflects your goodness to others. Amen."*

ACKNOWLEDGEMENTS

*This book is dedicated to Sandra Keith,
who inspired me years ago to write.
Also to Pastor Dale Frankum, who directed
my path and has gone with the Lord.
Pastor Ron Hogan, who has always
encouraged me, and still stands beside me
no matter what, through all my ups and
downs. This book is possible because of the
life you instilled in me.
I could name many more, but through the
years, there are just so many, and if you're
one of them, thank you.
Thank you all.*

ABOUT FRANCISCO CORTEZ

Francisco Cortez is head minister of Shackles to Freedom. He holds a Pastoral Development License with Grace International and is a certified Christian counselor through Destiny Bible College. He lives with his wife in Gulf Coast Texas.

A Note to the Prisoner & the Addict

To the incarcerated, to the drug addict, to the hustler and the struggler—you are a child of God.

There are plenty of religious people, your own brothers and sisters, who will try to keep you down. But God Himself will elevate you for His glory. He doesn't need you to have a degree, He doesn't need you to be perfect.

Jesus washed the sinners' feet.

Living a Christ-like life, though, you will be tested. It takes time, work, sacrifice, and submission.

When you fall, what will you do? Allow people to break you down, or by the will of God in you, will you get back up and keep going?

MATTHEW 25:34-40 (NIV)

34 "[...] 'Come, you who are blessed by my Father; take your inheritance, the kingdom prepared for you. 35 For I was hungry and you gave me something to eat, I was thirsty and you gave me something to drink, I was a stranger and you invited me in, 36 I needed clothes and you clothed me, I was sick and you looked after me, I was in prison and you came to visit me.' 37 Then the righteous

will answer him, 'Lord, when did we see you hungry and feed you, or thirsty and give you something to drink? **38** When did we see you a stranger and invite you in, or needing clothes and clothe you? **39** When did we see you sick or in prison and go to visit you?' **40** The King will reply, 'Truly I tell you, whatever you did for one of the least of these brothers and sisters of mine, you did for me.'"

9 798886 936515 6